ALCHEMICAL CATECHISM

PARACELSUS

Translator: A.E. Waite

Dalcassian
Publishing
Company
PHILADELPHIA, PA

ALCHEMICAL CATECHISM

All rights reserved. No part of the material protected by this copyright may be reproduced or utilized in any form, electronic or mechanical, including photocopying, recording or by any information storage and retrieval system, without written permission from the copyright owner.

Library of Congress Cataloging-in-Publication Data

Copyright © 2020 Dalcassian Publishing Co.
All rights reserved.

ALCHEMICAL CATECHISM

ALCHEMICAL CATECHISM

ALCHEMICAL CATECHISM

A SHORT CATECHISM OF ALCHEMY

Q. What is the chief study of a Philosopher?
A. It is the investigation of the operations of Nature.

Q. What is the end of Nature?
A. God, Who is also its beginning.

Q. Whence are all things derived?
A. From one and indivisible Nature.

Q. Into how many regions is Nature separated?
A. Into four palmary regions.

Q. Which are they?
A. The dry, the moist, the warm, and the cold, which are the four elementary qualities, whence all things originate.

Q. How is Nature differentiated?
A. Into male and female.

Q. To what may we compare Nature?
A. To Mercury.

Q. Give a concise definition of Nature.
A. It is not visible, though it operates visibly; for it is simply a volatile spirit, fulfilling its office in bodies, and animated by the universal spirit-the divine breath, the central and universal fire, which vivifies all things that exist.

Q. What should be the qualities possessed by the examiners of Nature?
A. They should be like unto Nature herself. That is to say, they should be truthful, simple, patient, and persevering.

Q. What matters should subsequently engross their attention?
A. The philosophers should most carefully ascertain whether their designs are in harmony with Nature, and of a possible and attainable kind; if they would accomplish by their own power anything that is usually performed by the power of Nature, they must imitate her in every detail.

Q. What method must be followed in order to produce something which shall be developed to a superior degree than Nature herself develops it.
A. The manner of its improvement must be studied, and this is invariably operated by means of a like nature. For example, if it be desired to develop the intrinsic virtue of a given metal beyond its natural condition, the chemist

ALCHEMICAL CATECHISM

must avail himself of the metallic nature itself, and must be able to discriminate between its male and female differentiations.

Q. Where does the metallic nature store her seeds?
A. In the four elements.

Q. With what materials can the philosopher alone accomplish anything?
A. With the germ of the given matter; this is its elixir or quintessence, more precious by far, and more useful, to the artist, than is Nature herself. Before the philosopher has extracted the seed, or germ, Nature, in his behalf, will be ready to perform her duty.

Q. What is the germ, or seed, of any substance?
A. It is the most subtle and perfect decoction and digestion of the substance itself; or, rather, it is the Balm of Sulphur, which is identical with the Radical Moisture of Metals.

Q. By what is this seed, or germ, engendered?
A. By the four elements, subject to the will of the Supreme Being, and through the direct intervention of the imagination of Nature.

Q. After what manner do the four elements operate?
A. By means of an incessant and uniform motion, each one, according to its quality, depositing its seed in the centre of the earth, where it is subjected to action and digested, and is subsequently expelled in an outward direction by the laws of movement.

Q. What do the philosophers understand by the centre of the earth?
A. A certain void place where nothing may repose, and the existence of which is assumed.

Q. Where, then, do the four elements expel and deposit their seeds?
A. In the ex-centre, or in the margin and circumference of the centre, which, after it has appropriated a portion, casts out the surplus into the region of excrement, scoriae, fire, and formless chaos.

Q. Illustrate this teaching by an example.
A. Take any level table, and set in its centre a vase filled with water; surround the vase with several things of various colours, especially salt, taking care that a proper distance intervenes between them all. Then pour out the water from the vase, and it will flow in streams here and there; one will encounter a substance of a red colour, and will assume a tinge of red; another will pass over the salt, and will contract a saline flavour; for it is certain that water does not modify the places which it traverses, but the diverse characteristics of places change the nature of water. In the same way the seed which is

deposited by the four elements at the centre of the earth is subject to a variety of modifications in the places through which it passes, so that every existing substance is produced in the likeness of its channel, and when a seed on its arrival at a certain point encounters pure earth and pure water, a pure substance results, but the contrary in an opposite case.

Q. After what manner do the elements procreate this seed?
A. In order to the complete elucidation of this point, it must be observed that there are two gross and heavy elements and two that are volatile in character. Two, in like manner, are dry and two humid, one out of the four being actually excessively dry, and the other excessively moist. They are also masculine and feminine. Now, each of them has a marked tendency to reproduce its own species within its own sphere. Moreover, they are never in repose, but are perpetually interacting, and each of them separates, of and by itself, the most subtle portion thereof. Their general place of meeting is in the centre, even the centre of the Archeus, that servant of Nature, where coming to mix their several seeds, they agitate and finally expel them to the exterior.

Q. What is the true and the first matter of all metals?
A. The first matter, properly so called, is dual in its essence, or is in itself of a twofold nature; one, nevertheless, cannot create a metal without the concurrence of the other. The first and the palmary essence is an aerial humidity, blended with a warm air, in the form of a fatty water, which adheres to all substances indiscriminately, whether they are pure or impure.

Q. How has this humidity been named by Philosophers?
A. Mercury.

Q. By what is it governed?
A. By the rays of the Sun and Moon.

Q. What is the second matter?
A. The warmth of the earth -otherwise, that dry heat which is termed Sulphur by the Philosophers.

Q. Can the entire material body be converted into seed?
A. Its eight-hundredth part only-that, namely, which is secreted in the centre of the body in question, and may, for example, be seen in a grain of wheat.

Q. Of what use is the bulk of the matter as regards its seed?
A. It is useful as a safeguard against excessive heat, cold, moisture, or aridity, and, in general, all hurtful inclemency, against which it acts as an envelope.

Q. Would those artists who pretend to reduce the whole matter of any body into seed derive any advantage from the process, supposing it were possible

to perform it?
A. None; on the contrary, their labour would be wholly unproductive, because nothing that is good can be accomplished by a deviation from natural methods.

Q. What, therefore, should be done?
A. The matter must be effectively separated from its impurities, for there is no metal, how pure soever, which is entirely free from imperfections, though their extent varies. Now all superfluities, cortices, and scoriae must be peeled off and purged out from the matter in order to discover its seed.

Q. What should receive the most careful attention of the Philosopher?
A. Assuredly, the end of Nature, and this is by no means to be looked for in the vulgar metals, because, these having issued already from the hands of the fashioner, it is no longer to be found therein.

Q. For what precise reason?
A. Because the vulgar metals, and chiefly gold, are absolutely dead, while ours, on the contrary, are absolutely living, and possess a soul.

Q. What is the life of metals?
A. It is no other substance than fire, when they are as yet imbedded in the mines.

Q. What is their death?
A. Their life and death are in reality one principle, for they die, as they live, by fire, but their death is from a fire of fusion.

Q. After what manner are metals conceived in the womb of the earth?
A. When the four elements have developed their power or virtue in the centre of the earth, and have deposited their seed, the Archeus of Nature, in the course of a distillatory process, sublimes them superficially by the warmth and energy of the perpetual movement.

Q. Into what does the wind resolve itself when it is distilled through the pores of the earth?
A. It resolves itself into water, whence all things spring; in this state it is merely a humid vapour, out of which there is subsequently evolved the principiated principle of all substances, which also serves as the first matter of the Philosophers.

Q. What then is this principiated principle, which is made use of as the first matter by the Children of Knowledge in the philosophic achievement?
A. It is this identical matter, which, the moment it is conceived, receives a permanent and unchangeable form.

ALCHEMICAL CATECHISM

Q. Are Saturn, Jupiter, Mars, Venus, the Sun, the Moon, etc., separately endowed with individual seed?
A. One is common to them all; their differences are to be accounted for by the: locality from which they are derived, not to speak of the fact that Nature completes her work with far greater rapidity in the procreation of silver than in that of gold, and so of the other metals, each in its own proportion.

Q. How is gold formed in the bowels of the earth?
A. When this vapour, of which we have spoken, is sublimed in the centre of the earth, and when it has passed through warm and pure places, where a certain sulphureous grease adheres to the channels, then this vapour, which the Philosophers have denominated their Mercury, becomes adapted and joined to this grease, which it sublimes with itself; from such amalgamation there is produced a certain unctuousness, which, abandoning the vaporous form, assumes that of grease, and is sublimised in other places, which have been cleansed by this preceding vapour, and the earth whereof has consequently been rendered more subtle, pure, and humid; it fills the pores of this earth, is joined thereto, and gold is produced as a result.

Q. How is Saturn engendered?
A. It occurs when the said unctuosity, or grease, passes through places which are totally impure and cold.

Q. How is Venus brought forth?
A. She is produced in localities where the earth itself is pure, but is mingled with impure sulphur.

Q. What power does the vapour, which we have recently mentioned, possess in the centre of the earth?
A. By its continual progress it has the power of perpetually rarefying whatsoever is crude and impure, and of successively attracting to itself all that is pure around it.

Q. What is the seed of the first matter of all things?
A. The first matter of things, that is to say, the matter of principiating principles is begotten by Nature, without the assistance of any other seed; in other words, Nature receives the matter from the elements, whence it subsequently brings forth the seed.

Q. What, absolutely speaking, is therefore the seed of things?
A. The seed in a body is no other thing than a congealed air, or a humid vapour, which is useless except it be dissolved by a warm vapour.

ALCHEMICAL CATECHISM

Q. How is the generation of seed comprised in the metallic kingdom?
A. By the artifice of Archeus the four elements, in the first generation of Nature, distil a ponderous vapour of water into the centre of the earth ; this is the seed of metals, and it is called Mercury, not on account of its essence, but because of its fluidity, and the facility with which it will adhere to each and every thing.

Q. Why is this vapour compared to sulphur?
A. Because of its internal heat.

Q. From what species of Mercury are we to conclude that the metals are composed?
A. The reference is exclusively to the Mercury of the Philosophers, and in no sense to the common or vulgar substance, which cannot become a seed, seeing that, like other metals, it already contains its own seed.

Q. What, therefore, must actually be accepted as the subject of our matter?
A. The seed alone, otherwise the fixed grain, and not the whole body, which is differentiated into Sulphur, or living male, and into Mercury, or living female.

Q. What operation must be afterwards performed
A. They must be joined together, so that they may form a germ, after which they will proceed to the procreation of a fruit which is conformed to their nature.

Q. What is the part of the artist in this operation?
A. The artist must do nothing but separate that which is subtle from that which is gross.

Q. To what, therefore, is the whole philosophic combination reduced?
A. The development of one into two, and the reduction of two into one, and nothing further.

Q. Whither must we turn for the seed and life of meals and minerals?
A. The seed of minerals is properly the water which exists in the centre And the heart of the minerals.

Q. How does Nature operate by the help of Art?
A. Every seed, whatsoever its kind, is useless, unless by Nature or Art it is placed in a suitable matrix, where it receives its life by the coction of the germ! and by the congelation of the pure particle, or fixed grain.

Q. How is the seed subsequently nourished and preserved?
A. By the warmth of its body.

ALCHEMICAL CATECHISM

Q. What is therefore performed by the artist in the mineral kingdom?
A. He finishes what cannot be finished by Nature on account of the crudity of the air, which has permeated the pores of all bodies by its violence, but on the surface and not in the bowels of the earth.

Q. What correspondence have the metals among themselves?
A. It is necessary for a proper comprehension of the nature of this correspondence to consider the position of the planets, and to pay attention to Saturn, which is the highest of all, and then is succeeded by Jupiter, next by Mars, the Sun, Venus, Mercury, and, lastly, by the Moon. It must be observed that the influential virtues of the planets do not ascend but descend, and experience teaches us that Mars can be easily converted into Venus, not Venus into Mars, which is of a lower sphere. So, also, Jupiter can be easily transmuted into Mercury, because Jupiter is superior to Mercury, the one being second after the firmament, the other second above the earth, and Saturn is highest of all, while the Moon is lowest. The Sun enters into all, but it is never ameliorated by its inferiors. It is clear that there is a large correspondence between Saturn and the Moon, in the middle of which is the Sun; but to all these changes the Philosopher should strive to administer the Sun.

Q. When the Philosophers speak of gold and silver, from which they extract their matter, are we to suppose that they refer to the vulgar gold and silver?
A. By no means; vulgar silver and gold are dead, while those of the Philosophers are full of life.

Q. What is the object of research among the Philosophers?
A. Proficiency in the art of perfecting what Nature has left imperfect in the mineral kingdom, and the attainment of the treasure of the Philosophical Stone.

Q. What is this Stone?
A. The Stone is nothing else than the radical humidity of the elements, perfectly purified and educed into a sovereign fixation, which causes it to perform such great things for health, life being resident exclusively in the humid radical.

Q. In what does the secret of accomplishing this admirable work consist?
A. It consists in knowing how to educe from potentiality into activity the innate warmth, or the fire of Nature, which is enclosed in the centre of the radical humidity.

Q. What are the precautions which must be made use of to guard against failure in the work?

ALCHEMICAL CATECHISM

A. Great pains must be taken to eliminate excrements from the matter, and to conserve nothing but the kernel, which contains all the virtue of the compound.

Q. Why does this medicine heal every species of disease?
A. It is not on account of tile variety of its qualities, but simply because it powerfully fortifies the natural warmth, which it gently stimulates, while other physics irritate it by too violent an action.

Q How can you demonstrate to me the truth of the art in the matter of the tincture?
A. Firstly, its truth is founded on the fact that the physical powder, being composed of the same substance as the metals, namely, quicksilver, has the faculty of combining with these in fusion, one nature easily embracing another which is like itself. Secondly, seeing that the imperfection of the base metals is owing to the crudeness of their quicksilver, and to that alone, the physical powder, which is a ripe and decocted quicksilver, and, in itself a pure fire, can easily communicate to them its own maturity, and can transmute them into its nature, after it has attracted their crude humidity, that is to say, their quicksilver, which is the sole substance that transmutes them, the rest being nothing but scoriae and excrements, which are rejected in projection.

Q. What road should the Philosopher follow that he may attain to the knowledge and execution of the physical work?
A. That precisely which was followed by the Great Architect of the Universe in the creation of the world, by observing how the chaos was evolved.

Q. What was the matter of the chaos?
A. It could be nothing else than a humid vapour, because water alone enters into all created substances, which all finish in a strange term, this term being a proper subject for the impression of all forms.

Q. Give me an example to illustrate what you have just stated.
A. An example may be found in the special productions of composite substances, the seeds of which invariably begin by resolving themselves into a certain humour, which is the chaos of the particular matter, whence issues, by a kind of irradiation, the complete form of the plant. Moreover, it should be observed that Holy Scripture makes no mention of anything except water as the material subject whereupon the Spirit of God brooded, nor of anything except light as the universal form of things.

Q. What profit may the Philosopher derive from these considerations, and what should he especially remark in the method of creation which was pursued by the Supreme Being?

ALCHEMICAL CATECHISM

A. In the first place he should observe the matter out of which the world was made; he will see that out of this confused mass, the Sovereign Artist began by extracting light, that this light in the same moment dissolved the darkness which covered the face of the earth, and that it served as the universal form of the matter. He will then easily perceive that in the generation of all composite substances, a species of irradiation takes place, and a separation of light and darkness, wherein Nature is an undeviating copyist of her Creator. The Philosopher will equally understand after what manner, by the action of this light, the empyrean, or firmament which divides the superior and inferior waters, was subsequently produced; how the sky was studded with luminous bodies; and how the necessity for the moon arose, which was owing to the space intervening between the things above and the things below; for the moon is an intermediate torch between the superior and the inferior worlds, receiving the celestial influences and communicating them to the earth. Finally he will understand how the Creator, in the gathering of the waters, produced dry land.

Q. How many heavens can you enumerate?
A. Properly there is one only, which is the firmament that divides the waters from the waters. Nevertheless, three are admitted, of which the first is the space that is above the clouds. In this heaven the waters are rarefied, and fall upon the fixed stars, and it is also in this space that the planets and wandering stars perform their revolutions. The second heaven is the firmament of the fixed stars, while the third is the abode of the supercelestial waters.

Q. Why is the rarefaction of the waters confined to the first heaven?
A. Because it is in the nature of rarefied substances to ascend, and because God, in His eternal laws, has assigned its proper sphere to everything.

Q. Why does each celestial body invariably revolve about an axis?
A. It is by reason of the primeval impetus which it received, and by virtue of the same law which will cause any heavy substance suspended from a thread to turn with the same velocity, if the power which impels its motion be always equal.

Q. Why do the superior waters never descend?
A. Because of their extreme rarefaction. It is for this reason that a skilled chemist can derive more profit from the study of rarefaction than from any other science whatsoever.

Q. What is the matter of the firmament?
A. It is properly air, which is more suitable than water as a medium of light.

ALCHEMICAL CATECHISM

Q. After the separation of the waters from the dry earth, what was performed by the Creator to originate generation?
A. He created a certain light which was destined for this office; He placed it in the central fire, and moderated this fire by the humidity of water and by the coldness of earth, so as to keep a check upon its energy and adapt it to His design.

Q. What is the action of this central fire?
A. It continually operates upon the nearest humid matter, which it exalts into vapour; now this vapour is the mercury of Nature and the first matter of the three kingdoms.

Q. How is the sulphur of Nature subsequently formed?
A. By the interaction of the central fire and the mercurial vapour.

Q. How is the salt of the sea produced?
A. By the action of the same fire upon aqueous humidity, when the aerial humidity, which is contained therein, has been exhaled.

Q. What should be done by a truly wise Philosopher when he has once mastered the foundation and the order in the procedure of the Great Architect of the Universe in the construction of all that exists in Nature?
A. He should, as far as may be possible, become a faithful copyist of his Creator. In the physical chaos he should make his chaos such as the original actually was; he should separate the light from the darkness : he should form his firmament for the separation of the waters which are above from the waters which are below, and should successively accomplish, point by point, the entire sequence of the creative act.

Q. With what is this grand and sublime operation performed?
A. With one single corpuscle, or minute body, which, so to speak, contains nothing but faeces, filth, and abominations, but whence a certain tenebrous and mercurial humidity is extracted, which contains in itself all that is required by the Philosopher, because, as a fact, he is in search of nothing hut the true Mercury.

Q. What kind of mercury, therefore, must he make use of in performing the work? A. Of a mercury which, as such, is not found on the earth, but is extracted from bodies, yet not from vulgar mercury, as it has been falsely said.

Q. Why is the latter unfitted to the needs of our work?
A. Because the wise artist must take notice that vulgar mercury has an insufficient quantity of sulphur, and he should consequently operate upon a

body created by Nature, in which Nature herself has united the sulphur and mercury that it is the work of the artist to separate.

Q. What must he subsequently do?
A. He must purify them and join them anew together.

Q. How do you denominate the body of which we have been speaking?
A. The RUDE STONE, Or Chaos, or Iliaste, or Hyle--that confused mass which is known but universally despised.

Q. As you have told me that Mercury is the one thing which the Philosopher must absolutely understand, will you give me a circumstantial description of it, so as to avoid misconception?
A. In respect of its nature, our Mercury is dual--fixed and volatile; in regard to its motion, it is also dual, for it has a motion of ascent and of descent; by that of descent, it is the influence of plants, by which it stimulates the drooping fire of Nature, and this is its first office previous to congelation. By its ascensional movement, it rises, seeking to be purified, and as this is after congelation, it is considered to be the radical moisture of substances, which, beneath its vile scoriae, still preserves the nobility of its first origin.

Q. How many species of moisture do you suppose to be in each composite thing?
A. There are three--the Elementary, which is properly the vase of the other elements; the Radical, which, accurately speaking, is the oil, or balm, in which the entire virtue of the subject is resident--lastly, the Alimentary, the true natural dissolvent, which draws up the drooping internal fire, causing corruption and blackness by its humidity, and fostering and sustaining the subject.

Q. How many species of Mercury are there known to the Philosophers?
A. The Mercury of the Philosophers may be regarded under four aspects; the first is entitled the Mercury of bodies, which is actually their concealed seed; the second is the Mercury of Nature, which is the Bath or Vase of the Philosophers, otherwise the humid radical; to the third has been applied the designation, Mercury of the Philosophers, because it is found in their laboratory and in their minera. It is the sphere of Saturn; it is the Diana of the Wise; it is the true salt of metals, after the acquisition of which the true philosophic work may be truly said to have begun. In its fourth aspect, it is called Common Mercury, which yet is not that of the Vulgar, but rather is properly the true air of the Philosophers, the true middle substance of water, the true secret and concealed fire, called also common fire, because it is common to all minerae, for it is the substance of metals, and thence do they derive their quantity and quality.

ALCHEMICAL CATECHISM

Q. How many operations art comprised in our work?
A. There is one only, which may be resolved into sublimation, and sublimation, according to Geber, is nothing other than the elevation of the dry matter by the mediation of fire, with adherence to its own vase.

Q. What precaution should be taken in reading the Hermetic Philosophers?
A. Great care, above all, must be observed upon this point, lest what they say upon the subject should be interpreted literally and in accordance with the mere sound of the words: For the letter killeth, but the spirit giveth life.

Q. What books should be read in order to have an acquaintance with our science?
A. Among the ancients, all the works of Hermes should especially be studied; in the next place, a certain book, entitled The Passage of the Red Sea, and another, The Entrance into the Promised Land. Paracelsus also should be read before all among elder writers, and, among other treatises, his Chemical Pathway, or the Manual of Paracelsus, which contains all the mysteries of demonstrative physics and the most arcane Kabbalah. This rare and unique manuscript work exists only in the Vatican Library, but Sendivogius had the good fortune to take a copy of it, which has helped in the illumination of the sages of our order. Secondly, Raymond Lully must be read, and his Vade Mecum above all, his dialogue called the Tree of Life, his testament, and his codicil. There must, however, be a certain precaution exercised in respect to the two last, because, like those of Geber, and also of Arnold de Villanova, they abound in false recipes and futile fictions, which seem to have been inserted with the object of more effectually disguising the truth from the ignorant. In the third place, the Turba Philosophorum which is a collection of ancient authors, contains much that is materially good, though there is much also which is valueless. Among mediaeval writers Zachary, Trevisan, Roger Bacon, and a certain anonymous author, whose book is entitled The Philosophers, should be held especially high in the estimation of the student. Among moderns the most worthy to be prized are John Fabricius, Francois de Nation, and Jean D'Espagnet, who wrote Physics Restored, though, to say the truth, he has imported some false precepts and fallacious opinions into his treatise.

Q. When may the Philosopher venture to undertake the work?
A. When he is, theoretically, able to extract, by means of a crude spirit, a digested spirit out of a body in dissolution, which digested spirit he must again rejoin to the vital oil.

Q. Explain me this theory in a clearer manner.
A. It may be demonstrated more completely in the actual process; the great experiment may be undertaken when the Philosopher, by the medium of a

ALCHEMICAL CATECHISM

vegetable menstruurn, united to a mineral menstruum, is qualified to dissolve a third essential menstruum, with which menstruums united he must wash the earth, and then exalt it into a celestial quintessence, to compose the sulphureous thunderbolt, which instantaneously penetrates substances and destroys their excrements.

Q. Have those persons a proper acquaintance with Nature who pretend to make use of vulgar gold for seed, and of vulgar mercury for the dissolvent, or the earth in which it should be sown?
A. Assuredly not, because neither the one nor the other possesses the external agent--gold, because it has been deprived of it by decoction, and mercury because it has never had it.

Q. In seeking this auriferous seed elsewhere than in gold itself, is there no danger of producing a species of monster, since one appears to be departing from Nature?
A. It is undoubtedly true that in gold is contained the auriferous seed, and that in a more perfect condition than it is found in any other body; but this does not force us to make use of vulgar gold, for such a seed is equally found in each of the other metals, and is nothing else but that fixed grain which Nature has infused in the first congelation of mercury, all metals having one origin and a common substance, as will be ultimately unveiled to those who become worthy of receiving it by application and assiduous study.

Q. What follows from this doctrine?
A. It follows that, although the seed is more perfect in gold, it may be extracted much more easily from another body than from gold itself, other bodies being more open, that is to say, less digested, and less restricted in their humidity.

Q. Give me an example taken from Nature.
A. Vulgar gold may be likened to a fruit which, having come to a perfect maturity, has been cut off from its tree, and though it contains a most perfect and well-digested seed, notwithstanding, should anyone set it in the ground, with a view to its multiplication, much time, trouble, and attention will be consumed in the development of its vegetative capabilities. On the other hand, if a cutting, or a root, be taken from the same tree, and similarly planted, in a short time, and with no trouble, it will spring up and produce much fruit.

Q. Is it necessary that an amateur of this science should understand the formation of metals in the bowels of the earth if he wishes to complete his work ?
A. So indispensable is such a knowledge that should anyone fail, before all

other studies, to apply himself to its attainment, and to imitate Nature point by point therein, he will never succeed in accomplishing anything but what is worthless.

Q. How, then, does Nature deposit metals in the bowels of the earth, and of what does she compose them?
A. Nature manufactures them all out of sulphur and mercury, and forms them by their double vapour.

Q. What do you mean by this double vapour, and how can metals be formed thereby?
A. In order to a complete understanding of this question, it must first be stated that mercurial vapour is united to sulphureous vapour in a cavernous place which contains a saline water, which serves as their matrix. Thus is formed, firstly, the Vitriol of Nature; secondly, by the commotion of the elements, there is developed out of this Vitriol of Nature a new vapour, which is neither mercurial nor sulphureous, yet is allied to both these natures, and this, passing through places to which the grease of sulphur adheres, is joined therewith, and out of their union a glutinous substance is produced, otherwise, a formless mass, which is permeated by the vapour that fills these cavernous places. By this vapour, acting through the sulphur it contains, are produced the perfect metals, provided that the vapour and the locality are pure. If the locality and the vapour are impure, imperfect metals result. The terms perfection and imperfection have reference to various degrees of concoction.

Q. What is contained in this vapour?
A. A spirit of light and a spirit of fire, of the nature of the celestial bodies, which properly should be considered as the form of the universe.

Q. What does this vapour represent?
A. This vapour, thus impregnated by the universal spirit, represents, in a fairly complete way, the original Chaos, which contained all that was required for the original creation, that is, universal matter and universal form.

Q. And one cannot, notwithstanding, make use of vulgar mercury in the process?
A. No, because vulgar mercury, as already made plain, is devoid of external agent.

Q. Whence comes it that common mercury is without its external agent?
A. Because in the exaltation of the double vapour, the commotion has been so great and searching, that the spirit, or agent, has evaporated, as occurs, with very close similarity, in the fusion of metals. The result is that the unique

ALCHEMICAL CATECHISM

mercurial part is deprived of its masculine or sulphureous agent, and consequently can never be transmuted into gold by Nature.

Q. How many species of gold are distinguished by the Philosophers?
A. Three sorts :--Astral Gold, Elementary Gold, and Vulgar Gold.

Q. What is astral gold?
A. Astral Gold has its centre in the sun, which communicates it by its rays to all inferior beings. It is an igneous substance, which receives a continual emanation of solar corpuscles that penetrate all things sentient, vegetable, and mineral.

Q. What do you refer to under the term Elementary Gold ?
A. This is the most pure and fixed portion of the elements, and of all that is composed of them. All sublunary beings included in the three kingdoms contain in their inmost centre a precious grain of this elementary gold.

Q. Give me some description of Vulgar Gold ?
A. It is the most beautiful metal of our acquaintance, the best that Nature can produce, as perfect as it is unalterable in itself.

Q. Of what species of gold is the Stone of the Philosophers ?
A. It is of the second species, as being the most pure portion of all the metallic elements after its purification, when it is termed living philosophical gold. A perfect equilibrium and equality of the four elements enter into the Physical Stone, and four things are indispensable for the accomplishment of the work, namely, composition, allocation, mixture, and union, which, once performed according to the rules of art, will beget the lawful Son of the Sun, and the Phoenix which eternally rises out of its own ashes.

Q. What is actually the living gold of the Philosophers?
A. It is exclusively the fire of Mercury, or that igneous virtue, contained in the radical moisture, to which it has already communicated the fixity and the nature of the sulphur, whence it has emanated, the mercurial character of the whole substance of philosophical sulphur permitting it to be alternatively termed mercury.

Q. What other name is also given by the Philosophers to their living gold ?
A. They also term it their living sulphur, and their true fire; they recognize its existence in all bodies, and there is nothing that can subsist without it.

Q. Where must we look for our living gold, our living sulphur, and our true fire ?
A. In the house of Mercury.

ALCHEMICAL CATECHISM

Q. By what is this fire nourished?
A. By the air.

Q. Give me a comparative illustration of the power of this fire?
A. To exemplify the attraction of this interior fire, there is no better comparison than that which is derived from the thunderbolt, which originally is simply a dry, terrestrial exhalation, united to a humid vapour. By exaltation, and by assuming the igneous nature, it acts on the humidity which is inherent to it; this it attracts to itself, transmutes it into its own nature, and then rapidly precipitates itself to the earth, where it is attracted by a fixed nature which is like unto its own.

Q. What should be done by the Philosopher after he has extracted his Mercury?
A. He should develop it from potentiality into activity.

Q. Cannot Nature perform this of herself?
A. No; because she stops short after the first sublimation, and out of the matter which is thus disposed do the metals engender.

Q. What do the Philosophers understand by their gold and silver?
A. The Philosophers apply to their Sulphur the name of Gold, and to their Mercury the name of Silver.

Q. Whence are they derived?
A. I have already stated that they are derived from a homogeneous body wherein they are found in great abundance, whence also Philosophers know how to extract both by an admirable, and entirely philosophical, process.

Q. When this operation has been duly performed, to what other point of the practice must they next apply themselves?
A. To the confection of the philosophical amalgam, which must be done with great care, but can only be accomplished after the preparation and sublimation of the Mercury.

Q. When should your matter be combined with the living gold?
A. During the period of amalgamation only, that is to say, Sulphur is introduced into it by means of the amalgamation, and thenceforth there is one substance; the process is shortened by the addition of Sulphur, while the tincture at the same time is augmented.

Q. What is contained in the centre of the radical moisture?
A. It contains and conceals Sulphur, which is covered with a hard rind.

ALCHEMICAL CATECHISM

Q. What must be done to apply it to the Great Work?
A. It must be drawn, out of its bonds with consummate skill, and by the method of putrefaction.

Q. Does Nature, in her work in the mines, possess a menstruum which is adapted to the dissolution and liberation of this sulphur?
A. No; because there is no local movement. Could Nature, unassisted, dissolve, putrefy, and purify the metallic body, she would herself provide us with !he Physical Stone, which is Sulphur exalted and increased in virtue.

Q. Can you elucidate this doctrine by an example?
A. By an enlargement of the previous comparison of a fruit, or a seed, which, in the first place, is put into the earth for its solution, and afterwards for its multiplication. Now, the Philosopher, who is in a position to discern what is good seed, extracts it from its centre, consigns it to its proper earth, when it has been well cured and prepared, and therein he rarefies it in such a manner that its prolific virtue is increased and indefinitely multiplied.

Q. In what does the whole secret of the seed consist ?
A. In the true knowledge of its proper earth.

Q. What do you understand by the seed in the work Of the Philosophers ?
A. I understand the interior heat, or the specific spirit, which is enclosed in the humid radical, which, in other words, is the middle substance of living silver, the proper sperm of metals, which contains its own seed.

Q. How do you set free the sulphur from its bonds?
A. By putrefaction.

Q. What is the earth of minerals ?
A. It is their proper menstruum.

Q. What pains must be taken by the Philosopher to extract that part which he requires?
A. He must take great pains to eliminate the fetid vapours and impure sulphurs, after which the seed must be injected.

Q. By what indication may the Artist be assured that he is in the right road at the beginning of his work?
A. When he finds that the dissolvent and the thing dissolved are converted into one form and one matter at the period of dissolution.

Q. How many solutions do you count in the Philosophic Work?
A. There are three. The first solution is that which reduces the crude and

metallic body into its elements of sulphur and of living silver; the second is that of the physical body, and the third is the solution of the mineral earth.

Q. How is the metallic body reduced by the first solution into mercury, and then into sulphur?
A. By the secret artificial fire, which is the Burning Star.

Q. How is this operation performed?
A. By extracting from the subject, in the first place, the mercury or vapour of the elements, and, after purification, by using it to liberate the sulphur from its bonds, by corruption, of which blackness is the indication.

Q. How is the second solution performed?
A. When the physical body is resolved into the two substances previously mentioned, and has acquired the celestial nature.

Q. What is the name which is applied by Philosophers to the Matter during this period?
A, It is called their Physical Chaos, and it is, in fact, the true First Matter, a name which can hardly be applied before the conjunction of the male--which is sulphur--with the female--which is silver.

Q. To what does the third solution refer?
A. It is the humectation of the mineral earth and it is closely bound up with multiplication.

Q. What fire must be made use of in our work?
A. That fire which is used by Nature.

Q. What is the potency of this fire?
A. It dissolves everything that is in the world, because it is the principle of all dissolution and corruption.

Q. Why is it also termed Mercury?
A. Because it is in its nature aerial, and a most subtle vapour, which partakes at the same time of sulphur, whence it has contracted some contamination.

Q. Where is this fire concealed?
A. It is concealed in the subject of art.

Q. Who is it that is familiar with, and can produce, this fire?
A. It is known to the wise, who can both produce it and purify it.

Q. What is the essential potency and characteristic of this fire?
A. It is excessively dry, and is continually in motion; it seeks only to

disintegrate and to educe things from potentiality into actuality; it is that, in a word, which coming upon solid places in mines, circulates in a vaporous form upon the matter, and dissolves it.

Q. How may this fire be most easily distinguished?
A. By the sulphureous excrements in which it is enveloped, and by the saline environment with which it is clothed.

Q. What must be added to this fire so as to accentuate its capacity for incineration in the feminine species?
A. On account of its extreme dryness it requires to be moistened.

Q. How many philosophical fires do you enumerate?
A. There are in all three--the natural, the unnatural, and the contra-natural.

Q. Explain to me these three species of fires.
A. The natural fire is the masculine fire, or the chief agent; the unnatural is the feminine, which is the dissolvent of Nature, nourishing a white smoke, and assuming that form. This smoke is quickly dissipated, unless much care be exercised, and it is almost incombustible, though by philosophical sublimation it becomes corporeal and resplendent. The contra-natural fire is that which disintegrates compounds and has the power to unbind what has' been bound very closely by Nature.

Q. Where is our matter to be found?
A. It is to be found everywhere, but it must specially be sought in metallic nature, where it is more easily available than elsewhere.

Q. What kind must be preferred before all others?
A. The most mature, the most appropriate, and the easiest; but care, before all things, must be taken that the metallic essence shall be present, not only potentially but in actuality, and that there is, moreover, a metallic splendour.

Q. Is everything contained in this subject?
A. Yes; but Nature, at the same time, must be assisted, so that the work may be perfected and hastened, and this by the means which are familiar to the higher grades of experiment.

Q. Is this subject exceedingly precious?
A. It is vile, and originally is without native elegance; should anyone say that it is saleable, it is the species to which they refer, but, fundamentally, it is not saleable, because it is useful in our work alone.

Q. What does our Matter contain?
A. It contains Salt, Sulphur, and Mercury.

ALCHEMICAL CATECHISM

Q. What operation is it most important to be able to perform?
A. The successive extraction of the Salt, Sulphur, and Mercury.

Q. How is that done ?
A. By sole and perfect sublimation.

Q. What is in the first place extracted ?
A. Mercury in the form of a white smoke.

Q. What follows?
A. Igneous water, or Sulphur.

Q. What then?
A. Dissolution with purified salt, in the first place volatilising that which is fixed, and afterwards fixing that which is volatile into a precious earth, which is the Vase of the Philosophers, and is wholly perfect.

Q. When must the Philosopher begin his enterprise ?
A. At the moment of daybreak, for his energy must never be relaxed.

Q. When may he take his rest?
A. When the work has come to its perfection.

Q. At what hour is the end of the work ?
A. High noon, that is to say, the moment when the Sun is in its fullest power, and the Son of the Day-Star in its most brilliant splendour.

Q. What is the pass-word of Magnesia?
A. You know whether I can or should answer:--I reserve my speech.

Q. Give me the greeting of the Philosophers.
A. Begin ; I will reply to you.

Q. Are you an apprentice Philosopher?
A. My friends, and the wise, know me.

Q. What is the age of a Philosopher ?
A. From the moment of his researches to that of his discoveries, the Philosopher does not age.

ALCHEMICAL CATECHISM

ALCHEMICAL CATECHISM

Phyſick Profeſſor(y) at Basil
Philip Theophraſtus PARACELSUS He died at
Saltzburge Anᵒ Dom: 1540. aged
47 yeares.
W. Marſhall ſculpsit

PARACELSUS (c. 1490 - 1541), the famous German physician of the 16th century, was probably born near Einsiedeln, in the canton Schwyz, in 1490 or 1491 according to some, or 1493 according to others. His father, the natural son of a grandmaster of the Teutonic order, was Wilhelm Bombast von Hohenheim, who had a hard struggle to make a subsistence as a physician. His mother was superintendent of the hospital at Einsiedeln, a post she relinquished upon her marriage. Paracelsus's name was Theophrastus Bombast von Hohenheim; for the names Philippus and Aureolus which are sometimes added good authority is wanting, and the epithet Paracelsus, like some similar compounds, was probably one of his own making, and was meant to denote his superiority to Celsus.

Of the early years of Paracelsus's life hardly anything is known. His father was his first teacher, and took pains to instruct him in all the learning of the time, especially in medicine. Doubtless Paracelsus learned rapidly what was put before him, but he seems at a comparatively early age to have questioned the value of what he was expected to acquire, and to have soon struck out ways for himself. At the age of sixteen he entered the university of Basel, but probably soon abandoned the studies therein pursued. He next went to J. Trithemius, the abbot of Sponheim and afterwards of Würzburg, under whom he prosecuted chemical researches. Trithemius is the reputed author of some obscure tracts on the great elixir, and as there was no other chemistry going Paracelsus would have to devote himself to the reiterated operations so characteristic of the notions of that time. But the confection of the stone of the philosophers was too remote a possibility to gratify the fiery spirit of a youth like Paracelsus, eager to make what he knew, or could learn, at once available for practical medicine. So he left school chemistry as he had forsaken university culture, and started for the mines in Tirol owned by the wealthy family of the Fuggers. The sort of knowledge he got there pleased him much more. There at least he was in contact with reality. The struggle with nature before the precious metals could be made of use impressed upon him more and more the importance of actual personal observation. He saw all the mechanical difficulties that had to be overcome in mining; he learned the nature and succession of rocks, the physical properties of minerals, ores and metals; he got a notion of mineral waters; he was an eyewitness of the accidents which befell the miners, and studied the diseases which attacked them; he had proof that positive knowledge of nature was not to be got in schools and universities, but only by going to nature herself, and to those who were constantly engaged with her. Hence came Paracelsus's peculiar mode of study. He attached no value to mere scholarship; scholastic disputations he utterly ignored and despised—and especially the discussions on medical topics, which turned more upon theories and definitions than upon actual practice. He therefore went wandering over a great part of Europe to learn all that he could. In so doing he was one of the first physicians of modern times to profit by a mode of study which is now reckoned indispensable. The book of nature, he affirmed, is that which the physician must read, and to do so he must walk over the leaves. The humours and passions and diseases of different nations are different, and the physician must go among the nations if he will be master of his art; the more he knows of other nations, the better he will understand his own. And the commentary of his own and succeeding centuries upon these very extreme views is that Paracelsus was no scholar, but an ignorant vagabond. He himself, however, valued his method and his knowledge very differently, and argued that he knew what his predecessors were ignorant of, because he had been taught in no human school. "Whence have I all my secrets, out of what writers and authors? Ask rather how the beasts have learned their arts. If nature can instruct irrational animals, can it not much more men?" In this new school discovered by Paracelsus, and since attended with the happiest results by many others, he remained for about ten years. He had acquired great stores of facts, which it was impossible for him to have reduced to order, but which gave him an unquestionable superiority to his contemporaries. So in 1526 or 1527, on his return to Basel, he was appointed town physician, and shortly afterwards he gave a course of lectures on medicine in the university. Unfortunately for him, the lectures broke away from tradition. They were in German, not in Latin; they were expositions of his own experience, of his own views, of his own methods of curing, adapted to the diseases that afflicted the Germans in the year 1527, and they were not commentaries on the text of Galen or Avicenna. They attacked, not only these great authorities, but the German graduates who followed them and disputed about them in 1527. They criticized in no measured terms the current medicine of the time, and exposed the practical ignorance, the pomposity, and the greed of those who practised it.

The truth of Paracelsus's doctrines was apparently confirmed by his success in curing or mitigating diseases for which the regular physicians could do nothing. For about a couple of years his reputation and practice increased to a surprising extent. But at the end of that time people began to recover themselves. Paracelsus had burst upon the schools with such novel views and methods, with such irresistible criticism, that all opposition was at first crushed flat. Gradually the sea began to rise. His enemies watched for slips and failures; the physicians maintained that he had no degree, and insisted that he should give proof of his qualifications. Moreover, he had a pharmaceutical system of his own which did not harmonize with the commercial arrangements of the apothecaries, and he not only did not use up their drugs like the Galenists, but, in the exercise of his functions as town physician, he urged the authorities to keep a sharp eye on the purity of their wares, upon their knowledge of their art, and upon their transactions with their friends the physicians. The growing jealousy and enmity culminated in a dispute with Canon Cornelius von Lichtenfels, who, having called in Paracelsus after other physicians had given up his case, refused to pay the fee he had promised in the event of cure; and, as the judges, to their discredit, sided with the canon, Paracelsus had no alternative but to tell them his opinion of the whole case and of their notions of justice. So little doubt left he on the subject that his friends judged it prudent for him to leave Basel at once, as it had been resolved to punish him for the attack on the authorities of which he had been guilty. He departed in such haste that he carried nothing with him, and some chemical apparatus and other property were taken charge of by J. Oporinus (1507—1568), his pupil and amanuensis. He went first to Esslingen, where he remained for a brief period, but had soon to leave from absolute want. Then began his wandering life, the course of which can be traced by the dates of his various writings. He thus visited in succession Colmar, Nuremberg, Appenzell, Zurich, Pfäffers, Augsburg, Villach, Meran, Middelheim and other places, seldom staying a twelvemonth in any of them. In this way he spent some dozen years, till 1541, when he was invited by Archbishop Ernst to settle at Salzburg, under his protection. After his endless tossing about, this seemed a promise and place of repose. It proved, however, to be the complete and final rest that he found, for after a few months he died, on the 24th of September. The cause of his death, like most other details in his history, is uncertain. His enemies asserted that he died in a low tavern in consequence of a drunken debauch of some days' duration. Others maintain that he was thrown down a steep place by some emissaries either of the physicians or of the apothecaries, both of whom he had during his life most grievously harassed. He was buried in the churchyard of St Sebastian, but in 1752 his bones were removed to the porch of the church, and a monument of reddish-white marble was erected to his memory.

The first book by Paracelsus was printed at Augsburg in 1529. It is entitled Practica D. Theophrasti Paracelsi, gemacht auff Europen, and forms a small quarto pamphlet of five leaves. Prior to this, in 1526 - 1527, appeared a programme of the lectures he intended to deliver at Basel, but this can hardly be reckoned a specific work. During his lifetime fourteen works and editions ware published, and thereafter, between 1542 and 1845, there were at least two hundred and thirty-four separate publications according to Mook's enumeration. The first collected edition was made by Johann Huser in German. It was printed at Basel in 1589 - 1591, in eleven volumes quarto, and is the best of all the editions. Huser did not employ the early printed copies only, but collected all the manuscripts which he could procure, and used them also in forming his text. The only drawback is that rather than omit anything which Paracelsus may have composed, he has gone to the opposite extreme and included writings with which it is pretty certain Paracelsus had nothing to do. The second collected German edition is in four volumes folio, 1603—1605. Parallel with it in 1603 the firstcollected Latin edition was made by Palthenius. It is in eleven volumes quarto, and was completed in 1605. Again, in 1616 - 1618 appeared a reissue of the folio German edition of 1603, and finally in 1658 came the Geneva Latin version, in three volumes folio, edited by Bitiskius.

The works were originally composed in Swiss-German, a vigorous speech which Paracelsus wielded with unmistakable power. The Latin versions were made or edited by Adam von Bodenstein, Gerard Dorn, Michael Toxites and Oporinus, about the middle of the 16th century. A few translations into other languages exist, as of the Chirurgia magna and some other works into French, and of one or two into Dutch, Italian and even Arabic. The translations into English amount to about a dozen, dating mostly from the middle of the 17th century. The original editions of Paracelsus's works are getting less and less common; even the English versions are among the rarest of their class. Over and above the numerous editions, there is a bulky literature of an explanatory and controversial character, for which the world is indebted to Paracelsus's followers and enemies. A good deal of it is taken up with a defence of chemical, or, they were called, "spagyric," medicines against the attacks of the supporters of the Galenic pharmacopoeia.

The aim of all Paracelsus's writing is to promote the progress of medicine, and he endeavours to put before physicians a grand ideal of their profession. In his attempts he takes the widest view of medicine. He bases it on the general relationship which man bears to nature as a whole; he cannot divorce the life of man from that of the universe; he cannot think of disease otherwise than as a phase of life. He is compelled, therefore, to rest his medical practice upon general theories of the present state of things; his medical system - if there is such a thing - is an adaptation of his cosmogony. It is this latter which has been the stumbling-block to many past critics of Paracelsus, and unless its character is remembered it will be the same to others in the future. Dissatisfied with the Aristotelianism of his time, Paracelsus turned with greater expectation to the Neoplatonism which was reviving. His eagerness to understand the relationship of man to the universe led him to the Kabbala, where these mysteries seemed to be explained, and from these unsubstantial materials he constructed, so far as it can be understood, his visionary philosophy. Interwoven with it, however, were the results of his own personal experience and work in natural history and chemical pharmacy and practical medicine, unfettered by any speculative generalizations, and so shrewd an observer as Paracelsus was must have often felt that his philosophy and his experience did not agree with one another. Some of his doctrines are alluded to in the article MEDICINE (q.v.), and it would serve no purpose to give even a brief sketch of his views, seeing that their influence has passed entirely away, and that they are of interest only in their place in a general history of medicine and philosophy. Defective, however, as they may have been, and unfounded in fact, his kabbalistic doctrines led him to trace the dependence of the human body upon outer nature for its sustenance and cure. The doctrine of signatures, the supposed connexion of every part of the little world of man with a corresponding part of the great world of nature, was a fanciful and false exaggeration of this doctrine, but the idea carried in its train that of specifics. This led to the search for these, which were not to be found in the bewildering and untested mixtures of the Galenic prescriptions. Paracelsus had seen how bodies were purified and intensified by chemical operations, and he thought if plants and minerals could be made to yield their active principles it would surely be better to employ these than the crude and unprepared originals. He had besides arrived by some kind of intuition at the conclusion that the operations in the body were of a chemical character, and that when disordered they were to be put right by counter operations of the same kind. It may be claimed for Paracelsus that he embraced within the idea of chemical action something more than the alchemists did. Whether or not he believed in the philosopher's elixir is of very little consequence. If he did, he was like the rest of his age; but he troubled himself very little, if at all, about it. He did believe in the immediate use for therapeutics of the salts and other preparations which his practical skill enabled him to make. Technically he was not a chemist; he did not concern himself either with the composition of his compounds or with an explanation of what occurred in their making. If he could get potent drugs to cure disease he was content, and he worked very hard in an empirical way to make them. That he found out some new compounds is certain; but not one great and marked discovery can be ascribed to him. Probably, therefore, his positive services are to be summed up in this wide application of chemical ideas to pharmacy and therapeutics; his indirect and possibly greater services are to be found in the stimulus, the revolutionary stimulus, of his ideas about method and general theory. It is most difficult to appreciate aright this man of fervid imagination, of powerful and persistent convictions, of unbated honesty and love of truth, of keen insight into the errors (as he thought them) of his time, of a merciless will to lay bare these errors and to reform the abuses to which they gave rise, who in an instant offends us by his boasting, his grossness, his want of self-respect. It is a problem how to reconcile his ignorance, his weakness, his superstition, his crude notions, his erroneous observations, his ridiculous influences and theories, with his grasp of method, his lofty views of the true scope of medicine, his lucid statements, his incisive and epigrammatic criticisms of men and motives. Sea Marx, Zur Würdigung des Theophrastus von Hohenheim (Göttingen, 1842); Mook, Theophrastus Paracelsus, eine kritische Studie (Würzburg, 1876); Hartman, Life of P. T. Paracelsus (London, 1887); Schubert und Sudhoff, Paracelsus-Forschungen (Frankfurt a.M., 1887—1889); Sudhoff, Versuch einer Kritik der Echtheit der Paracelsischen Schriften (Berlin, 1894); Waite, The Hermetic and Alchemical Writings of Paracelsus (London, 1894).

www.ingramcontent.com/pod-product-compliance
Lightning Source LLC
LaVergne TN
LVHW021746060526
838200LV00052B/3499